**Name** »» _____

**I'm with** »» _____

# In the Backseat

**And we're going to** »» _____

**KNOCK KNOCK**®
VENICE, CALIFORNIA

**Draw where you're going!**

1. Find your starting city.
2. Now, find your ending city.
3. Connect the two places with a line.
4. If you know where you'll be stopping along the way, add those places, too!

**WHAT YOU NEED:**

- Pencil
- Eraser
- Notebook (for game scores and tallies)
- Black marker
- Crayons or colored pencils
- Pair of dice
- Adhesive tape or glue
- Safety scissors (for the vomit bag, page 27)

# »Are we there yet?»

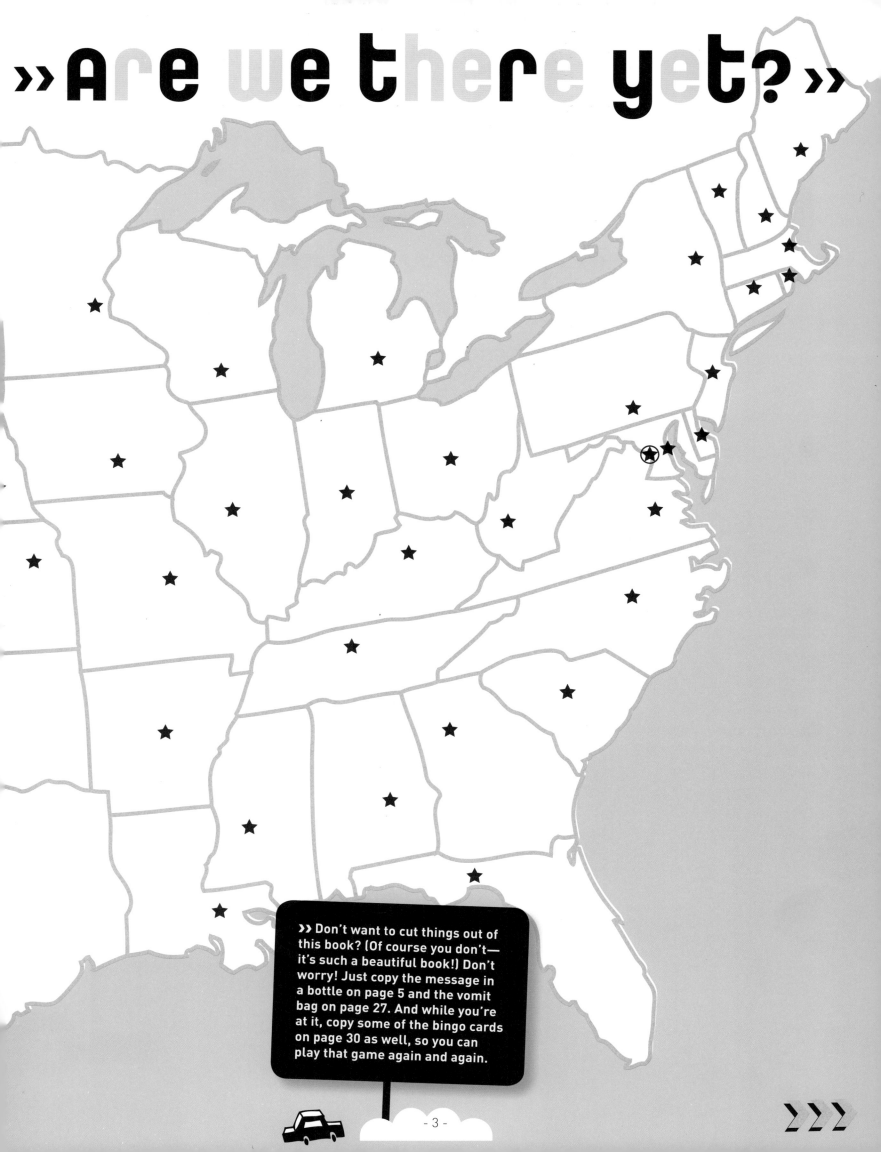

> **>> Don't want to cut things out of this book? (Of course you don't— it's such a beautiful book!) Don't worry! Just copy the message in a bottle on page 5 and the vomit bag on page 27. And while you're at it, copy some of the bingo cards on page 30 as well, so you can play that game again and again.**

# LET'S GET ROLLING

Roll the dice and add up the numbers to see what you have to do!

**2** Ask everybody in the car to think of a fruit. Then, try to guess which fruit each person picked. If you get 'em all right, you might be a mind reader!

**3** Start laughing now and don't stop until you see a red car (or until your stomach starts to hurt).

**4** Whisper, "How much wood can a woodchuck chuck?" five times in a row as fast as you can.

**5** Make a fart noise. Now sing, "Toot, toot! Ah, beep, beep!" three times in a row.

**6** Tell your fellow passengers a funny story. It must include a duck, a trumpet, a rotten egg, and a truck driver.

**7** Open and close your window three times in a row and murmur, "I'm just crazy about rotten bananas on toast!"

**8** You're in love with the car. Give the window a big kiss. Aw, so romantic!

**9** Say something nice about everybody in the car. Then shout, "JUST KIDDING! No really, seriously I'm serious."

**10** Wiggle your body and say, "I have organiflexi-vegetarian chicken thighs and chicken legs."

**11** You've just won the Most Awesome Person in the Car Award! Proclaim your award by declaring, "I'm king of the car! I have tiger's blood and guts of glory."

**12** Imitate the animal you hope to be in your next life.

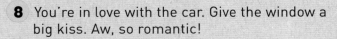

# message in a bottle

find a clear plastic bottle. (There might be one on the floor of the car!) Cut out this page and write your message. You can write a juicy secret, a letter to an imaginary friend, or a helpful tip, like "Don't order the soup here. It's disgusting!" Roll your message up tightly and insert it into the bottle. Then, pick a place to leave your message for someone else to find. With luck, they'll follow the instructions and pass it on to another lucky person!

You can leave your message in a bottle at a restaurant, gas station, or a rest stop. Or ask a store clerk if you can leave it on the counter.

Don't want to cut up this book? Then copy this page or just take the whole page out!

## message in a bottle

P.S. If you find this message in a bottle, please continue its journey. Write your own message on the back, and leave it along your path for someone else to find!

FROM:

(You can also fill this out with an alias, if needed, such as "Sillypants the Magnificent.")

I, (name)

Found this message in a bottle on (date)

At (the place where you found it)

This is how I noticed the message in a bottle:

This is what I thought when I opened the bottle:

This is what I want to write to the next person who receives this:

**Beep beep!**

Stump yourself—and everyone else in the car!

**1** Mary's father has three daughters; the oldest is April and the youngest is June. What's the name of his second daughter?

**a.** May
**b.** July
**c.** You can't know that.
**d.** Mary

**2** Valerie thought it was very nice that Avery and Maeve invited her to go to the movies.

How many "v"s are in this sentence?

**a.** 4
**b.** 5
**c.** 6
**d.** 1

**3** What's a frizzle?

**a.** A kind of fowl
**b.** A bad hairstyle
**c.** A crazy-looking plant
**d.** A frothy drink

**4** How many days start with the letter "t"?

**a.** 4
**b.** 2
**c.** 1
**d.** 3

**5** What's red and white and goes through the woods at a speed of 800 mph?

**a.** Jed, the puking gnome
**b.** John, the kissing gnome
**c.** Jane, the racing gnome
**d.** Jo, the breakdancing gnome

**6** What's brown and sticky?

**a.** Melted vanilla ice cream
**b.** Moldy food
**c.** Coffee
**d.** A stick

**7** Which is heaviest?

**a.** A ton of cotton balls
**b.** A ton of cement
**c.** A ton of pickles
**d.** There's no difference.

**8** Henry has a drawer with twenty socks; ten black and ten blue. He wakes up very early in the morning, and keeps the lights off so he won't wake his brother Howard. How many socks does Henry have to take out of the drawer, to make sure he has two socks of the same color?

**a.** 2
**b.** 10
**c.** 3
**d.** 20

**9** What do you give a lion for his birthday?

**a.** A sweater
**b.** A sandwich
**c.** A skateboard
**d.** I don't know, but you'd better hope he likes it!

See page 32 for the answers!

# FI⯅⯅ me!

- [ ] 33 Cars
- [ ] 1 Police car
- [ ] 1 Race car
- [ ] 2 Ambulances
- [ ] 2 Buses
- [ ] 1 Tank
- [ ] 1 Trailer
- [ ] 1 Sphinx
- [ ] 4 Pyramids
- [ ] 1 Hot-air balloon
- [ ] 11 Trees
- [ ] 4 Tulips
- [ ] 2 Traffic lights
- [ ] 1 Dog poop
- [x] 7 Tent pins
- [ ] 1 Airplane
- [ ] 3 Traffic signs
- [x] 2 Ghosts
- [ ] 1 Ghostdriver
- [ ] 3 Cyclists
- [ ] 1 Man with mustache
- [ ] 2 Ski jumps
- [ ] 8 Buildings
- [ ] 3 Coins
- [ ] 1 Astronaut
- [ ] 1 Flaming hoop
- [ ] 2 Dogs
- [ ] 9 Cows
- [ ] 1 Lost sheep
- [x] 4 Gnomes
- [ ] 1 Man in a bathing suit
- [ ] 2 Cherries
- [ ] 9 Tents
- [x] 1 Little man with a mushroom hat

# BACK-SEAT
## GAMES

## Yellow Car

Yellow cars are relatively rare. When you spot one, yell out, "Yellow car!" and earn a point.

## Mine!

Divide the cars that are driving on the other side of the road. The first car that passes is yours, the second one is for your brother or sister (or whomever is in the car with you), the third one is for the driver, and so on, then you start over again. You'll celebrate when a fancy sports car passes an old clunker at the last moment, and you get that sweet ride instead of your brother. This game doesn't have points—it's just fun!

## Driver Says

The driver commands, in random order, things like "Driver says, hold your hands up high!" or "Driver says, wiggle your feet!" and so on. You have to follow the command, but only if the phrase "Driver says" is used. So, if the driver says, "Open your mouth!" and you do it, you're out. Last one left wins a point.

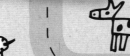
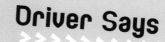

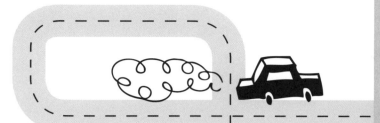

## Annoying Noises

<<<<<<<<<<<<<<<<

Take turns making annoying noises. For example, try burping or blowing raspberries. The person who makes someone else laugh first is the winner and gets one point!

## Guard the Border

>>>>>>>>>>>>>>>>

Make an imaginary wall between you and the other players. When someone crosses into your territory and you catch them, you get a point!

## Hold Your Breath

>>>>>>>>>>>>>>>

Hold your breath when you cross a bridge or go through a tunnel. (Make sure you don't hold it too long!) If you can hold your breath the whole time, you get a point.

## A to Z

>>>>>>>>>>>>>>>>>

Look for words on signs (letters on license plates do not count). Start with the letter A. So, if you see the word "Area," you can continue and look for words starting with the letter B. Whoever reaches the letter Z first wins. You can skip the letters J, Q, and X. (You can also play together for fun and try to find the alphabet as fast as possible without having a winner.)

**The backseat is the best seat!**

## Birds Have Feathers

>>>>>>>>>>>>>>>>>>>>>>>>>>>>>>>>

The driver of the car should say something like "Parrots have feathers," and then everybody has to flap their arms as if they were wings. If the driver calls out something that doesn't have feathers, like "Eggs have feathers," you should not flap your arms. If you do, you're out. Whoever's still in at the end of the game wins a point.

## Fortunately/Unfortunately

>>>>>>>>>>>>>>>>>>>>>

Tell a story together. Everyone takes a turn saying a sentence that starts "Fortunately . . ." or "Unfortunately . . ." If you don't like the story anymore, you can always opt for a terrible ending, such as "Unfortunately, the universe exploded, and nothing was left." In this game, there are no winners or losers—just chuckles!

## Yes or No

<<<<<<<<<<<<<<<<<<<<<<<<

Whisper strange commands to your fellow passengers, and then ask the driver to say "yes" or "no" to you. (Make sure your whispers are extra quiet, so the driver doesn't know what they are.) For example, whisper, "Make a funny face at the car next to us!" to the person sitting closest to you. If the driver says, "Yes," the other person must do it. If the driver says, "No," the other person is off the hook. You don't get points in this game, just lots of craziness!

## I'm Not Touching You

<<<<<<<<<<<<<<<<<<<<<<<

Put your hands or your face as close as possible to the other person in the backseat, with only just enough room left for one hair. Your backseat partner will tell you to stop, and then you can say, "I didn't touch you!" And that's one point.

## Rain, Rain

>>>>>>>>>>>>>>>>

Each person in the car chooses a raindrop on the window. The raindrop that reaches the bottom of the window first wins one point for its owner.

## License Plates

>>>>>>>>>>>>>>>>>>>>

Choose a license plate and pretend the letters on it stand for words that describe the people in the car (or in your car). For instance, if there's a license plate with a Y, an A, and an S, you could say it stands for "You Are Silly!"

## Car-Car-Spaceship!

>>>>>>>>>>>>>>>>>>>>

When you say, "start!" the next three vehicles you see are yours, the three vehicles after that are for the next player, and so on. Car-car-car isn't worth much, but car-car-truck will get you some real points. And if you see a spaceship . . . you're the winner!

## Car-Car-Spaceship!
### Points

| | Points |
|---|---|
| car car car | = 1 |
| car car truck | = 10 |
| truck truck truck | = 30 |
| truck car car | = 10 |
| car car car | = 5 |
| truck truck car | = 20 |
| car limo limo | = 50 |
| limo limo limo | = 500 |
| limo car car | = 70 |
| car car convertible | = 60 |
| ambulance car car | = 250 |
| car car bus | = 150 |
| car car spaceship | = 1000 |

# FIND me!

<<<<<<<<<<<<<<

- ☐ 1 Mouse
- ☐ 13 Living trees
- ☐ 1 Broken tree
- ☐ 2 Ants
- ☐ 2 Snails
- ☐ 1 Cowboy boot
- ☐ 1 Slug
- ☐ 1 Half apple
- ☐ 1 Rainbow
- ☐ 3 Crosses
- ☐ 1 Frog
- ☐ 2 Gnomes
- ☐ 1 Blue man
- ☐ 1 Bird with pointy beak
- ☐ 1 Mummy
- ☐ 1 Startled hare with its ears up
- ☐ 4 Hungry ladybugs
- ☐ 1 Squirrel
- ☐ 1 Mustache
- ☐ 1 Piece of toast with legs
- ☐ 1 Octopus (actually a quadropus)
- ☐ 1 Fez (funny hat with a tassel)

- ☐ 1 Spider
- ☐ 1 Log
- ☐ 21 Houses
- ☐ 1 Karate master with black belt
- ☐ 6 Castles
- ☐ 2 Rockets
- ☐ 1 Church
- ☐ 2 UFOs
- ☐ 4 Flames
- ☐ 3 Coins
- ☐ 5 Lone arrows
- ☐ 2 Cherries
- ☐ 2 Tents
- ☐ 1 Sad duck in pond that's too small
- ☐ 9 Knights
- ☐ 3 Swords
- ☐ 1 Sheep

# COLOR me!

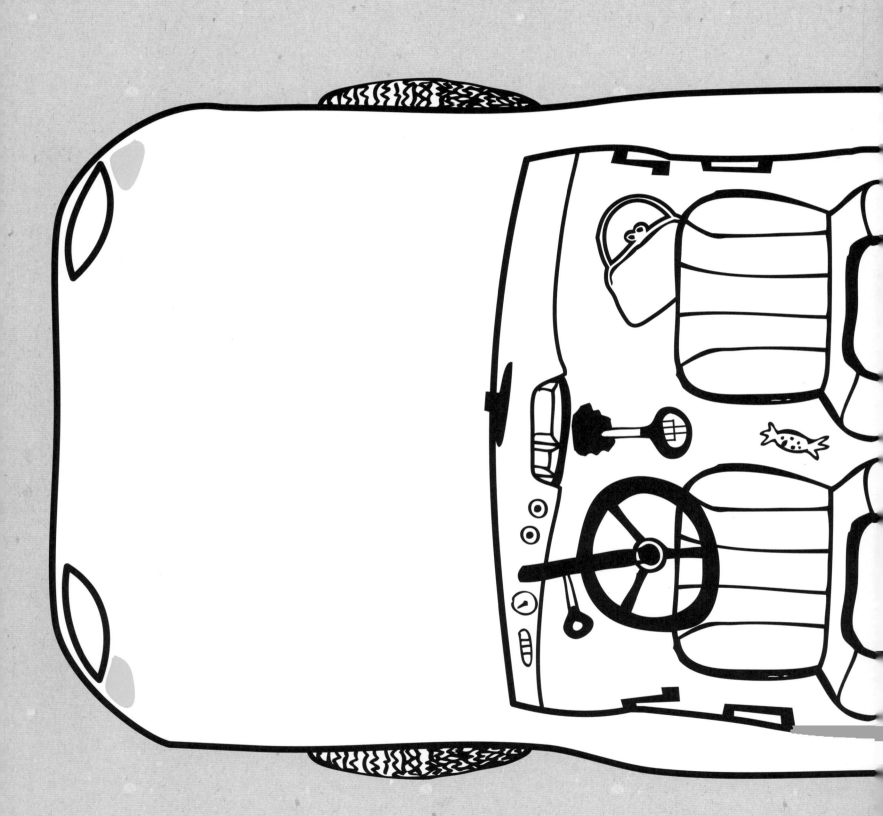

Use crayons or colored pencils to color in the car. Make sure to draw the people you are driving with and any trash or goodies that you have in the car. You might even want to add something you wish you had in the car, like an ice cream cone or a hippopotamus!

# LET'S GET ROLLING

Roll the dice and add up the numbers to see what you have to do!

**2** You have 30 seconds to make the passenger sitting closest to you laugh. Okay, go!

**3** Have an argument with yourself about what to order at the next fast-food place you pass.

**4** Your head isn't screwed on right. Hold it in place for the next two minutes or it'll fall off.

**5** Name three US states that begin with "New." (There are actually four total.)

**6** Pretend to lay a golden egg, then "crack" it (gently!) over another passenger's head.

**7** Make up a new dance called the Funky Monkey. Perform it in your seat until you get another driver to honk at you.

**8** Press your face against the window and make a weird face to the first passerby you see.

**9** Pick a random feature of the car and try to "sell" it to your fellow passengers.

**10** Serenade the driver with your favorite song or Broadway show tune.

**11** Give everyone in the car a funny (but not mean!) nickname that rhymes with his or her first or last name.

**12** Shout ". . . and I've got gas!" after everything you say for the next three minutes.

# DICTIONARY
## speak to me!

» The backseat is a great place to learn a language. Don't choose a common, boring language that millions of people already speak. You should learn the language of Luxembourgish, since not that many people speak it. (The only problem might be that nobody understands what you're saying!) «

**EN:** I want a cookie.
**LUX:** Ech wëll een kichelchen.

**EN:** Is it still far?
**LUX:** Ass et nach wäit?

**EN:** Are we there yet?
**LUX:** Sinn mer do?

**EN:** When are we going to stop?
**LUX:** Wéini kenne mer arretéieren?

**EN:** I want something to drink.
**LUX:** Ech wëll eppes drenken goen.

**EN:** I didn't do anything!
**LUX:** Ech mecht näischt!

**EN:** I didn't touch him!
**LUX:** Ech paaken hien net un!

**EN:** It wasn't me!
**LUX:** Dat war ech net!

**EN:** Five candy bars, please. My dad is paying.
**LUX:** Fënnef äis, wann ech gelift, mäin. Papp bezilt.

**EN:** Hello!
**LUX:** Moien!

**EN:** I have to go to the bathroom.
**LUX:** Ech muss kacken.

**EN:** Bathroom
**LUX:** Cabinet

**EN:** The pooper
**LUX:** Schäisshasichen

**EN:** I have to pee.
**LUX:** Ech muss pissen.

**EN:** Fool
**LUX:** Dabo

**EN:** Darn!
**LUX:** Nondikas!

**EN:** Slob
**LUX:** Topeg

**EN:** May I put this bottle on the counter?
**LUX:** Daerf ech d'Fläsch an d'Desch stellen?

# FIND me!

<<<<<<<<<<<<<<<<

- ☑ 38 Buildings
- ☑ 1 Eiffel Tower
- ☑ 11 Monkeys
- ☑ 1 Croissant
- ☑ 1 Butterfly
- ☐ 8 Cyclists
- ☑ 10 Bicycles
- ☑ 1 Helicopter
- ☐ 1 Book
- ☐ 2 Rockets
- ☑ 4 Ugly ducklings
- ☐ 3 Swans
- ☐ 2 Tents
- ☐ 3 Bananas / banana peels
- ☑ 1 Little man in a banana suit
- ☐ 1 Windmill
- ☐ 1 Newspaper
- ☑ 1 Funny little gnome man
- ☐ 1 Squirrel
- ☐ 1 Queen
- ☐ 1 Boot
- ☐ 4 Striped rodents
- ☐ 1 Bus stop
- ☐ 1 Frenchman
- ☐ 2 Mustaches
- ☐ 1 Loaf of bread
- ☐ 1 Mime, skating against the wind
- ☐ 1 Spinning wheel
- ☐ 1 Cup of coffee
- ☐ 1 Cow
- ☐ 1 Cyclist with polka-dot jersey

# RIDDLES and jokes

answers on page 32!

**1** Five little old ladies are in a room with a basket holding five apples. How can you give all the old ladies an apple and still leave one apple in the basket?

**a.** You give the last old lady the basket with one apple in it.
**b.** You put one old lady in the hallway.
**c.** You throw the apples in the trash can.
**d.** Old ladies don't even like apples.

**2** Which invention enables you to see through walls?

**a.** A transparent telescope
**b.** A window
**c.** X-ray spectacles
**d.** Sunglasses

**3** You're competing in a run. Right before the finish line, you pass the runner who is in second place. In which position do you finish?

**a.** First place
**b.** Second place
**c.** Last place
**d.** Third place

**4** How do you write in French?

**a.** You visit France.
**b.** You move to France.
**c.** You take French classes.
**d.** You use a pen.

**5** What does a vegetarian cannibal eat?

**a.** Nothing
**b.** Picklemakers
**c.** Carrots with ranch dressing
**d.** Vegetarian cannibals are extinct.

**6** Once upon a time, there was a man who bought hundreds of donuts daily for $1 a donut. He sold the donuts for 50 cents apiece. After selling donuts for years, he became a millionaire. How is that possible?

**a.** He was already a billionaire.
**b.** He didn't know how to count.
**c.** He didn't sell all the donuts.
**d.** Donuts started growing on trees.

**7** A man takes the train every day from New York to Washington, DC. This takes him two hours and fifty minutes, but the return trip takes 170 minutes. How is that possible?

**a.** The train all of a sudden went faster.
**b.** On the way back, it was a high-speed train.
**c.** Two hours and fifty minutes is just as long as 170 minutes.
**d.** There was a headwind.

**8** What has fifty eyes and two teeth?

**a.** A playground filled with babies
**b.** A non-existent monster
**c.** A shark family after a trip to the dentist
**d.** A jumping spider

# PIXEL ME!

Use crayons or colored pencils and draw anything you want— robots, rainbows, rhinos—in the blank grid space! (You can outline it first, one pixel at a time.)

# FIND me!

<<<<<<<<<<<<<<<

- ☐ 1 Planet
- ☐ 2 Dog poops
- ☐ 5 Badminton birdies
- ☐ 3 Badminton-playing blue men
- ☐ 16 Stars
- ☐ 1 Moon
- ☐ 6 Raindrops
- ☐ 1 Half apple
- ☐ 67 Ants
- ☐ 1 Man with no shirt
- ☐ 14 Tents
- ☐ 1 Gnome
- ☐ 2 Teepees
- ☐ 22 Acorns
- ☐ 3 Benches
- ☐ 22 Trees
- ☐ 4 Tulips
- ☐ 3 Slingshots
- ☐ 3 Trailers
- ☐ 1 Milkshake
- ☐ 5 Balloons
- ☐ 1 Squirrel
- ☐ 1 Teddy bear
- ☐ 1 Angry bear
- ☐ 1 Anteater
- ☐ 4 Fires
- ☐ 1 Ladybug

- ☐ 2 Snails
- ☐ 1 Wolf
- ☐ 1 Turtle
- ☐ 3 Ducks
- ☐ 1 Duck pond toy
- ☐ 1 Cyclist
- ☐ 1 Knight
- ☐ 2 Pigeons

# BARFacts

You barf because your brain gets confused. One part of your brain thinks it's not moving, but another part doesn't agree. Some people get sick more easily when they're reading during the drive, especially when they're reading something about being sick. Like now. Right this second. (Hint: Barf only if you really need to!)

## Anti-sickness tips:

- The smoother your parent drives, the smaller the chance that you'll get sick.
- Fresh and cool air may also help. Open a window or turn on the A/C.
- Make sure you don't have an empty stomach, but don't eat anything greasy or sour. Drink water instead of soft drinks.
- Whine that you want to sit in front. When it works and you're sitting in front, look ahead as far as possible.
- Keep your eyes closed the entire time.

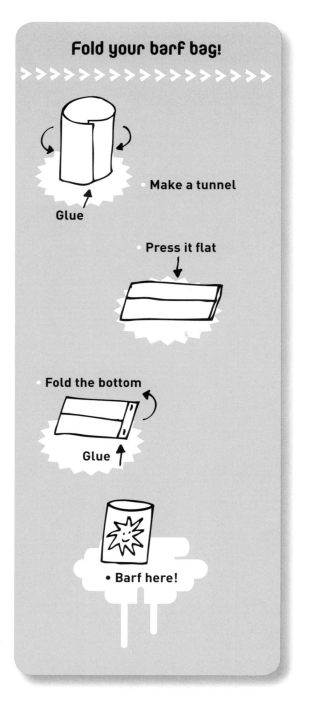

**Fold your barf bag!**

Make a tunnel

Glue

Press it flat

Fold the bottom

Glue

Barf here!

First, color in the vomit page and then vomit in the coloring page.

Fold the coloring page and make it into a nice little container. This may come in handy when you start feeling sick and suddenly need to throw up.

What goes down . . . sometimes comes up.

# backseat bingo!

**G**rownups often repeat themselves over and over (and over!). When one of the grownups in the car says one of the phrases on your bingo card, cross it out. The first person with a full card wins. The winner gets the Grownups Are Boring Award!

Don't want to cross out things in the book? Just copy the page. Or, create your own bingo cards filled with some of your family's favorite sayings.

Slow Down! Bingoooo!

# BINGO CARD 1 ⭐

| | | | |
|---|---|---|---|
| Look at that! | Can you turn it down, please!? | No, we're not getting ice cream. | Hey, use your turn signal! |
| Slow down! | Is your seat belt on? | I've been driving a long time—don't upset me. | Be quiet back there! |
| Shoot, missed the exit. | Look at the beautiful view! | Don't make me stop the car. | Did you hear me? |

# BINGO CARD 3 ⭐

| | | | |
|---|---|---|---|
| Watch your language! | Pay attention. | I've had enough. | What a great vacation! |
| Let your sister/brother sleep. | Please don't kick my seat. | Who said that? | Close the window. |
| Open the window. | No, you just had some candy. | No _____ I told you, no _____ in the car. | Don't make me pull over. |

# ☆ BINGO CARD 2 ☆

| | | | |
|---|---|---|---|
| Stop with that bingo game! | Can you please keep it down? | What's the speed limit here? | We're a few miles from _____. |
| Mmmm! | Parents never get vacations. | Well, I'm glad we're not stuck in that traffic jam! | We don't use that kind of language. |
| Leave your brother/sister alone. | Yes, it's still a long way. | Stop making those disgusting sounds. | Look how beautiful this is! |

# ☆ BINGO CARD 4 ☆

| | | | |
|---|---|---|---|
| I can't concentrate like this, kids! | People here don't know how to drive. | Was this our exit or is it the next one? | Now I want to listen to my music. |
| No, we're not there yet. | Aren't we lucky, kids? | Just let me drive my own way. | We'll stop soon. |
| Hey, hey, hey! | I need a bathroom break. | Leave each other alone! | You can only go ___ mph here. |

# RIDDLES AND JOKES ANSWERS

**ANSWERS PAGE 22**

1 a. You give the last old lady the basket with one apple in it.

2 b. A window

3 b. Second place

4 d. You use a pen.

5 b. Vegetarian cannibals are extinct.

6 a. He was already a billionaire.

7 c. Two hours and fifty minutes is just as long as 170 minutes.

8 d. A playground filled with babies

**ANSWERS PAGE 7**

1 d. Mary

2 d. 1

3 a. A kind of fowl

4 a. 4 (Tuesday, Thursday, today, and tomorrow)

5 c. Jane the racing gnome

6 d. A stick

7 d. There's no difference.

8 c. 3

9 d. I don't know, but you'd better hope he likes it!